HOW SCIENCE SAVED the EIFFEL TOWER

by Emma Bland Smith

illustrated by Lia Visirin

CAPSTONE EDITIONS

a capstone imprint

Bang!
Crash!
Clatter!

Balanced on platforms and
leaning on ladders, workers
pounded and hammered.

Day by day, as astonished Parisians watched, an iron tower climbed into the sky. When completed, the Eiffel Tower would be the tallest structure in the world!

Its creator, Gustave Eiffel, promised it would be *magnifique*.

But the people of Paris weren't so sure.

They pointed as they strolled down the busy boulevards.

"It looks like a metal asparagus!"
  said one Parisian.

"Buildings should be made of stone, not iron!"
  complained some.

"It's useless!" said others.

Thank goodness it's only temporary, they thought.

The 1,000-foot tower was going to mark the entrance for the 1889 World's Fair. Its three levels would be connected by elevators and winding stairs. It would house four fancy restaurants, a newspaper printing press, and a post office. At the very top level, there would be an apartment for Monsieur Eiffel himself.

And the tower would make the city money. Millions of people would visit Paris to see it! The officials agreed to let it remain for 20 years. But after that, they figured, it would be quite useless. In 1909, the tower would be torn down and sold for scrap metal.

The iron latticework continued to grow, beam by beam,
rivet by rivet.

It was so different, so *moderne*!

Too *moderne*, in fact, for many of the fine
people of Paris.

They protested!

Forty-seven artists and writers signed a letter,
expressing their dismay at this ridiculous tower.
They said it would make Paris the laughingstock
of the world.

Monsieur Eiffel read the letter with surprise. As much as these Parisians hated the building, Monsieur Eiffel adored it. He was an engineer who had spent a career constructing fine bridges. (He even built the interior framework for the Statue of Liberty!) The curved shape of the tower was brilliantly designed to withstand the greatest winds. Eiffel believed there was beauty in such an engineering feat. Its wondrous height and daring new style would be an homage to France, the country he loved.

"When it is finished, Parisians will love it!" he exclaimed.

In May 1889, the fair finally opened. People from all over the world flocked to the startling structure. What would they think?

Visitors stared at it from the ground—so graceful! Climbing the stairs, they admired the artistic ironwork—so *élégant*! From the top, they gazed at all of Paris and beyond—so breathtaking! The city shimmered. Few people had ever seen the world from this high.

Oh là là!

Monsieur Eiffel was right—people loved the tower! Even most of the artists and writers who had complained changed their mind after seeing the completed structure.

But one thing bothered Monsieur Eiffel. The city of Paris
was still planning to tear the tower down after the exhibition!
He needed to convince them that the tower should stay.

Alors, he came up with a plan.
He'd make his tower too useful to tear down.

Monsieur Eiffel had a passion for science. The tower, he decided, would be "an observatory and a laboratory such as science has never had at its disposal."

Could science save the Eiffel Tower?

Monsieur Eiffel got to work. He teamed up with the French weather bureau. Together they installed a state-of-the-art weather station on the third floor. They put another on the tiny platform on the tip-top of the tower. While people bought tickets and souvenirs on the ground floor, Monsieur Eiffel recorded temperatures, wind, and air pressure 900 feet in the sky. He graphed the results and sent measurements by cable to a nearby weather station.

Formidable! Now the weather service could compare measurements from as high as a mountain to those on the ground. They learned new and exciting information. For example, the temperature at the top of the tower was 2.3 degrees warmer than at the bottom. This groundbreaking data helped scientists give more accurate weather predictions.

Now would
the city keep
the tower?

Non?

Then he must do something
even more impressive.

The scientific world was just beginning to
experiment with flying. But they still hadn't figured
out the basic principles of how flight worked.

How did birds fly?
How could a heavy machine mimic them?

Monsieur Eiffel turned his tower into an aviation
and aerodynamics laboratory.

While tourists sent postcards from the third platform post office, Eiffel ran a cable from the second platform to the ground. He sent objects of varying size and weight flying down it. He measured their speed and took the air resistance into account. Then, he built a wind tunnel at the base of the tower to test airplane parts in a controlled environment. He published his findings.

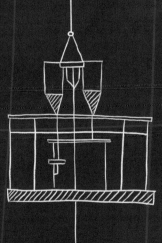

Intéressant! Scientists took note. From Monsieur Eiffel, they learned necessary information about two important aspects of flying: the way air flowed over wings, and the way a propeller worked. Eiffel's research helped the growing aviation industry take a huge step forward!

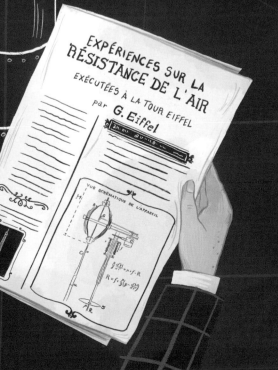

Now would the city agree to preserve the tower?

Still, the answer was *non*. In fact, some officials thought it should come down even sooner than planned! The city formed a committee to decide the tower's fate. The debate was fierce. Should the tower stay?

"*Oui!* It's innovative. It's inspirational. It's part of the skyline!"

"*Non!* It's ugly. It's dangerous. And the experiments are so noisy!"

Oui!

Non!

Oui!

Non!

Finally, they decided to keep it—for now.

Phew! Monsieur Eiffel was relieved. But he was more determined than ever to use science to permanently save his beloved tower. What else could he do?

Monsieur Eiffel pondered. He had one more idea up his sleeve.

Eiffel had already set up a wireless radio center on the top of the tower. In fact, the very first wireless message in France had been sent from there to a monument across Paris in 1898!

Now, Monsieur Eiffel wondered if he could get the French military interested in using his tower. For several years, the military had wanted to study ways to use this new wireless communication technology. They even tasked a young engineer with looking into the matter! There was just one *problème*: They didn't have any money to pay for the work.

So when Monsieur Eiffel offered them the use of his tower for their research, at no expense, they said . . .

Oui!

And the deal was made! Monsieur Eiffel had a wooden shack built near one of the tower's feet, fitted with cutting-edge equipment.

Zap!

The military practiced sending wireless messages from the antenna on the top of the tower. They reached places as far away as Germany, Morocco, and even North America!

They began to broadcast time signals twice a day. That helped ships at sea find their way safely. (Later, during World War I, the military even captured an important enemy message using the tower!)

The French military, like the aviation industry and the weather bureau, had come to depend on the Eiffel Tower.

Once again, a committee was formed. The members examined the facts. Not only did Parisians now love *la Tour Eiffel*, it had also become a beacon of science and technology.

It was no longer useless—it was *très, très* useful!
Too useful to tear down.

Monsieur Eiffel rejoiced. His tower was safe, forever.

Science had saved the Eiffel Tower!

Epilogue

Gustave Eiffel's contributions to the field of scientific research were significant, no mere hobby. The Eiffel Tower was arguably his greatest creation as a builder, and his last. He retired from his engineering firm in 1893. From then on, he spent most of his days atop his beloved tower, conducting thousands of experiments in meteorology, physics, radio transmission, and aviation. Eiffel died at age 91, in Paris.

French Terms Used

alors—so

élégant—elegant

formidable—wonderful

intéressant—interesting

magnifique—magnificent

moderne—modern

non—no

oh là là!—oh my! Wow!

oui—yes

problème—problem

très—very

More Interesting Facts about the Eiffel Tower

- Before the construction of the Eiffel Tower, the world's tallest structure was the Washington Monument, in the United States.
- Eiffel provided most of the funds for building the tower. In return, the city agreed to let him leave it up for 20 years, in order to earn back his investment. He made the money back in one year.
- The tower took only two years, two months, and five days to build. (The Washington Monument took 36 years.) The cost came in 6 percent under budget, and only one life was lost (compared to the tragic 25 lives lost in the construction of the Brooklyn Bridge).
- The tower required 18,000 metal pieces, 2,500,000 connector pieces called rivets, 7,300 tons of iron, and 60 tons of paint.
- The Eiffel Tower can sway nearly three inches in the wind and expand seven inches in the heat.
- Today, the tower's nickname is "The Iron Lady" ("*La Dame de Fer*").
- The Eiffel Tower remained the tallest building in the world until the completion of New York City's Chrysler Building in 1930.

Timeline

1832: Gustave Eiffel was born in Dijon, France.

1855: Eiffel originally planned to work in his uncle's vinegar factory in Dijon and earned a degree in chemical engineering. However, instead of pursuing that path, he found a job in a railway manufacturing business. There he learned about metal design and new building techniques.

1860: Eiffel took over and completed the management of a railway bridge project.

1862: Eiffel married Marie Gaudelet. They had five children. Marie died in 1887 and Eiffel never remarried. All his life he remained especially close to his daughter Claire, who, with her husband and children, lived with Eiffel in his Paris home.

1866: Eiffel set up his own engineering firm and railway bridge workshop.

1879–1883: Eiffel worked on the inner framework of the Statue of Liberty.

1882–1884: Eiffel designed and built the Garabit Viaduct, the world's tallest bridge at the time.

1887: Eiffel won a contest for the creation of a structure for the 1889 World's Fair. The drawings had originated with two of his employees, engineers Maurice Koechlin and Émile Nouguier. He had tasked them with coming up with a basic design for a 300-meter iron tower. From there, Eiffel took over, working with architect Stephen Sauvestre to make the structure attractive.

1889: The Eiffel Tower opened at the 1889 World's Fair. It was paid for largely by Eiffel himself.

1889–1913: Eiffel spent much time at the Eiffel Tower conducting scientific experiments.

1898: The first radio message in France was sent from the Eiffel Tower to the Panthéon monument.

1909: Eiffel built a wind tunnel at the foot of the tower. People later complained about its noise. He moved it to a suburb of Paris, where it exists to this day.

1923: Eiffel died in his house in Paris at age 91.

Dedication

For Roger Bland, great scientist and even greater dad. You and Eiffel would have been good pals. —EBS

To Marc, my little scientist: Follow your dreams, they will take you where you need to be. —LV

About the Author

Emma Bland Smith is a librarian and the award-winning author of thirteen books for children, including *The Gardener of Alcatraz* and *Claude: The True Story of a White Alligator*. Emma lived in Paris as a young adult and has always wanted to set a book in that beautiful city! Today, she lives in San Francisco with her family. Visit her online at emmabsmith.com.

About the Illustrator

Lia Visirin was born in a small town in Transylvania, Romania, where she now lives with her husband and many houseplants. She has a bachelor's degree in traditional graphic arts but is a self-taught children's book illustrator. Lia gets inspiration from nature, old photographs, and childhood memories, which transform into wonderfully whimsical illustrations.

Source Notes

page 10, line 9: Allwood, John. *The Great Exhibitions*. London: Cassell & Collier Macmillan, 1977, p. 77.
page 15, line 2-3: Harriss, Joseph. *The Tallest Tower: Eiffel and the Belle Epoque*. Boston: Houghton Mifflin, 1975, p. 102.

Selected Bibliography

Allwood, John. *The Great Exhibitions*. London: Cassell & Collier Macmillan, 1977.

Greene, Meg. *The Eiffel Tower*. San Diego: Lucent Books, 2001.

Harriss, Joseph. *The Tallest Tower: Eiffel and the Belle Epoque*. Boston: Houghton Mifflin, 1975.

Harvie, David I. *Eiffel: The Genius Who Reinvented Himself*. Thrup, Stroud: Sutton Publishing Limited, 2004.

Jonnes, Jill. *Eiffel's Tower: And the World's Fair Where Buffalo Bill Beguiled Paris, the Artists Quarreled, and Thomas Edison Became a Count*. New York: Viking, 2009.

Loyrette, Henri. *Gustave Eiffel*. Translated by Henri Loyrette. New York: Rizzoli, 1985.

Published by Capstone Editions, an imprint of Capstone
1710 Roe Crest Drive, North Mankato, Minnesota 56003
capstonepub.com

Text copyright © 2022 by Emma Bland Smith
Illustrations copyright © 2022 by Capstone

Library of Congress Cataloging-in-Publication Data is available on the Library of Congress website
ISBN: 9781684464784 (hardcover)
ISBN: 9781684469376 (paperback)
ISBN: 9781684465170 (ebook PDF)

Summary: The city of Paris planned to tear down the Eiffel Tower. But its builder, Gustave Eiffel, an engineer and amateur scientist, was determined to save it, and he crafted a clever plan to make the tower too scientifically useful to tear down. As the date for the tower's demolition approached, Eiffel raced to prove its worth. Could science save the Eiffel Tower?

Designed by Heidi Thompson

Printed and bound in China. 5593